W I L **G S!**

· · · · · · · · · · · · · · · · · ·

ppo

house

egan

elly Byrne

BLOOMSBURY
LONDON BERLIN NEW YORK SYDNEY

Published 2011 by
Bloomsbury Publishing PLC
49–51 Bedford Square, London, WC1B 3DP

www.bloomsbury.com

ISBN   HB 978-1-4081-4245-5
           PB 978-1-4081-5680-3

This book is produced using paper that is made from wood grown in managed, sustainable forests. It is natural, renewable and recyclable. The logging and manufacturing processes conform to the environmental regulations of the country of origin.

Produced for Bloomsbury Publishing by Calcium. www.calciumcreative.co.uk

Illustrated by Kelly Bryne

Picture acknowledgements: Shutterstock: Hallam Creations 23tr, Olga Miltsova 23tl.

Printed in China by Toppan Leefung

All the internet addresses given in this book were correct at the time of going to press. The author and publishers regret any inconvenience caused if addresses have changed or sites have ceased to exist, but can accept no responsibility for any such changes.

Contents

Ring, ring. Wild thing!

If you're WILD about animals, today's your lucky day.

There's a **pygmy hippo** at the door! You could invite it in...

Pygmy hippos might be smaller than **common hippos**, but they are still BIGGER than you.

Ouch!

5

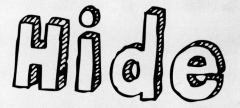

Hide

Pygmy hippos are clever animals.

You will need

a big garden

large bushes for your hippo to hide in

6

In the wild, they run and
hide instead of fighting.

Oops!

Hide and seek might
make a mess...

Cool

When it gets hot,
hippos need to chill!

They spend about
16 hours every
day staying
cool in a pool.

You will need

to dig a very big hole in
your lawn (and hope your
parents don't mind!)

loads of water

lots of water reeds

Huh?!

Sorry – your paddling
pool won't do!

Yuck

Watch out at toilet time,
it may get messy...

Pygmy hippos swirl their tail when they poo, and fling **muck** everywhere.

Gross!

Don't stand too close!

Heavy

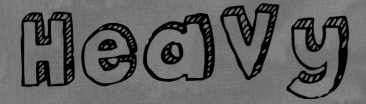

When they're fully grown, pygmy hippos are heavy.

They can weigh as much as four grown-up people!

Oof!

Better hide your
favourite toys...

13

Splash!

Bath time is a big deal for pygmy hippos. They LOVE it!

Pygmy hippos can close their ears and **nostrils** to hide under the water from **predators**.

You will need

towels (lots of them)

a HUGE bath

a book to read (while you're waiting for your hippo to scrub-a-dub)

PYGMY HIPPO POEMS

Pygmy hippos can hold their breath for seven minutes. Wow!

Don't panic!

Snooze

All clean and ready for bed – splat!

Did you know that pygmy hippos love to sleep in a pool of soft, squishy mud?!

You will need

soil

water

a shallow hole in the garden

16

This is one bed
you don't want
to share!

Zzzzz

Time to
go home

Your hippo seems happy, but your parents really aren't!

It's time to post your pet back to its real home...

A hamster makes a great pet, but a pygmy hippo is a WILD THING!

Cool creatures

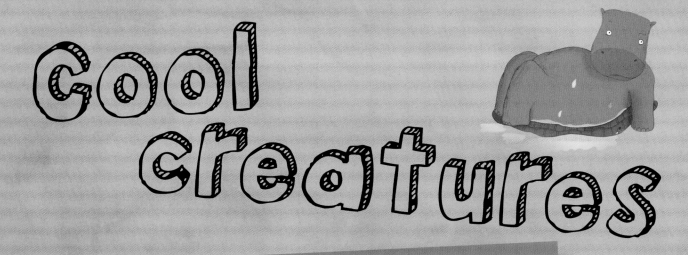

In the wild, pygmy hippos live in just a handful of countries on the west coast of Africa.

A pygmy hippo's mouth hides two giant teeth, called tusks.

Their skin looks shiny because it is covered in a kind of slime that acts like sunblock.

A pygmy hippo opens its mouth really wide, like a yawn. It may look like it is laughing, but it is probably trying to scare other creatures away.

Scientists think there are fewer than 3,000 pygmy hippos living in the wild today.

Glossary

common hippos *the type of hippo most often found in the wild. They are bigger than pygmy hippos*

disinfectant *a liquid that kills germs*

muck *animal poo*

nostrils *openings on an animal's head that allow it to breathe in air*

poachers *people who hunt animals that are protected by law*

predators *animals that hunt other animals for food*

pygmy hippo *a rare hippo that is smaller than a common hippo*

tusks *very long teeth*

Thanks for having me!

The Zoological Society of London (ZSL) is a charity that provides help for animals at home and worldwide. We also run ZSL London Zoo and ZSL Whipsnade Zoo.

By buying this book, you have helped us raise money to continue our work with animals around the world.

Find out more at zsl.org

23

Take them all home!

ISBN HB 978-1-4081-4247-9
      PB 978-1-4081-5678-0

ISBN HB 978-1-4081-4246-2
      PB 978-1-4081-5679-7

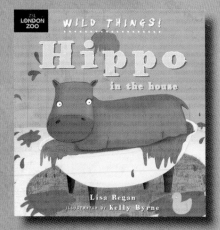

ISBN HB 978-1-4081-4245-5
      PB 978-1-4081-5680-3

ISBN HB 978-1-4081-4244-8
      PB 978-1-4081-5681-0